M000222211

A Noelia y
Sebastian

A Cage Within

por su
pareja
Caleidoscopica
su

Wulf

Copyright © 2012, Wendy Guerra
English Translation Copyright © 2012, 2013 by Elizabeth Polli
Introduction Copyright © 2012, 2013 by Peter Money

First Edition

ISBN 978-0-9882755-0-8

Harbor Mountain Press, Inc., is a 501(c)(3) organization dedicated to works
of high literary merit. Harbor Mountain Press books are distributed by
Small Press Distribution, a non-profit organization, through
GenPop Books and Distribution, and through our website.
The Press appreciates support.

Many thanks to Carina Pons and her agency for generous cooperation
in the publication of this volume.

Harbor Mountain Press acknowledges and thanks Ana Merino,
of the University of Iowa, Ernán López-Nussa, and our guides and friends
of Harbor Mountain Bel Esprit, for their generous spirit, in no small part,
for making this essential book possible.

SERIES EDITOR
Peter Money

MANAGING EDITOR
Partridge Boswell

DESIGN
Heron Graphic Arts

COVER ART
Bennett Bean
"Master #6.27, Body Language Series"
bennettbean.com

Harbor Mountain Press
PO Box 519
Brownsville, VT 05037

www.HarborMountainPress.org

A Cage Within

Poems by
Wendy Guerra

Translated by
Elizabeth Polli

Harbor Mountain Press
Vermont

Contents

Introduction

I first met Wendy Guerra's poems, two of them, in Welsh poet Richard Gwyn's translation. These two poems were so remarkable I began "teaching them" in my classes.

In early 2012 I prepared for a trip to Cuba (thank you, Vermont Caribbean Institute) by researching the history of Cuban literature, Cuban culture, history, geography, and articles existing from online controversy. I found myself reading the fine print of U.S. law and as many Cuban perspectives as I could absorb. One of the sites to which I returned frequently was the "Havana Cultura" index of artists, musicians, writers. The high quality biographical short films—jump-cut edited with pizzazz, interesting cinemagraphic angles, deft rhythmic soundtracks and interviews—brought me to Wendy Guerra. Her work was speaking to me in my tongue, a found sister of imagination, a sort of melancholic-exuberant, a kindred daydreamer of canvas and brushes, and as much her own. When Wendy Guerra described her work in the "Havana Cultura" segment (and in subsequent interviews I watched or read), she appeared to be articulating a new hybrid global language to which I related: one not troubled by rule or expectation, by syntax or subject, able to converse across wide expanses of impasse; a voltage for travelers who necessarily use a new lexicon—as they would respond to emerging sound. In other words: I read a liberator. Wendy Guerra's writing feels honest in a way only vulnerability can awaken, prescient visions harnessed wildly in the body of courage. I hear her like an open secret.

Almost immediately, I asked Ana Merino's U.S. translator, Elizabeth Polli, to read Guerra's poems. I was intoxicated on the gumbo nectar of what I came across and Polli's tender and sensitive experience with these translations emboldened her to this new text. We understand the groove continues beyond borders. Guerra is well known in Latin America and increasingly in Europe. Harbor Mountain Press is proud to bring you this first volume out of the United States. The time has come!

This volume marks the first appearance in the English-speaking continental West of an amazing writer whose gifts offer the allure of the metaphysical and the physical as though they were of the same body and strangers, both. Admirer (and translator) of Anais Nin, Wendy Guerra is herself a sort of descendant of Nin: where sensuality is the motivating instinct, where the reality of living is observed for the daily radical compromise that sustains our tensions, where surreality is the sour and sweet elixir that allows mind and body to unite and explode nakedly in speech and persona across borders and cosmos, where language is the nest and the rabbit hole for convictions and for raves, where opening one's mouth is a kind of dance and flame coming from stagnations and waves. A native of Cuba, Wendy Guerra writes for the 21st Century—writes for all centuries—like a kind of solitary roman candle, illumined by its own agreement with the dark. Guerra has everything to offer new readers: at once partly maker of film, scholar of distant things brought near, muse and curator of painted and visual curiosity, impresario of lost and found souls—both in sea-strewn linen and glittery heels. If heels be wings, *A Cage Within* may well be the moxie for every hand that holds a pen; a play of fusion to the confusion. The world just got bigger, and—through the haze that borders every interaction: more intimate.

—Peter Money

Ships that pass in the night, and speak each other in passing,

Only a signal shown and a distant voice in the darkness;

So on the ocean of life we pass and speak one another,

Only a look and a voice, then darkness again and a silence.

HENRY WADSWORTH LONGFELLOW

The cage has become bird
and it has flown
and my heart is crazy
because it howls to death
and behind the wind
at my deliriums [...]

ALEJANDRA PIZARNIK

A CAGE WITHIN

And she who is I wants to open the cage
cage that separates me from the living
But we were already   yes   a bit dead what with everything and birds hungry for light
Dead from all the words silenced in the darkness   you have reached us
Ready to predict from the learned confinement
I strive to translate with vigor my letters engraved on the body.

POEMS IN CHINESE

I rise every morning before anyone in the village
just to open the cage for the birds that you later hear sing
The night swallows them and silences with black velvet
it betrays you and I awake broken
opening cages   swallowing tears
exhaling the remains of my dead wings into the dawn.

My eyebrows were tattooed in Chinese and in a delicate fashion
Summer in the Orient belongs to that harsh dynastic and dry   dense pleasure
passions that explode in the dazzling light   poisonous and blind
I hold onto my distorted inheritance   trail of brief erotic sketches
lacey breasts
I fleetingly return there   to my Asiatic poverties of rice and Chinese ink
intimate sex
Women moan with desire
I call out your name in pain.

You know my dead and my gestures and my prayers to those dead whom you call by name
You offer them food and you serve my squalid body
that doesn't swallow that doesn't drink that doesn't sleep   that hasn't lived here for centuries
You name the bird and determine if it is free or a prisoner   by its trill
It is I who lives inside the heart of the bird
She who eats and drinks like the bird is the woman you touch and bless

Don't free me from the ritual that feeds your dead
and keeps me alive.

TOY CAGE

I see traps along the way
but they look like flowers   compasses or mirrors
The collection of cages I inherited from my mother made me female
I fell as low as the deep sound of my orchestra
That's where I'm going   arrogant and enslaved
The onslaught promises the worst
Girl   toy cage
My virgin heart   flushed   doesn't inherit insult or pain
And it's just that there are no cages inside the body of a girl.

A HOUSE WITHIN

There is no possible hiding place here
vanity or mirror
clear translucent structure
clean and deserted
on a small scale
A HOUSE WITHIN
of an uncomfortable rationalism
Japanese equilibrium of broken silk
unjust and icy outcome
without altars or flowers   without photos   without family
passing through and insomnia
patrimony and artifice
A HOUSE WITHIN
No one has gathered here
Not children Nor men Nor ideas.

BRIEF BIOGRAPHY OF RICE

Orphan
born and raised in Saigon
I've paid my way since childhood
Indigo keeps the heart of the lotus white
In certain photos I look like a western girl
they interrogate me when I row in the mangroves and sing the truths
My job is to separate the jasmine from the rice
my hobby is to draw you in silence
to erase the excess clothing on your body
You live naked in my silk diary
I follow the line with raised hand   I tear up my figure and dislodge you
All I have learned about bombs is read in the past
I'm old to be adopted and young to be crazy   I go on groping
I know my penance   kneeling and mute
thick silence   unknown and profitable
I cross vain words on my bicycle
my pedals are silver switchblades breaking the sound
The trail of rice marks the brief path I follow every day
I'm coming to take care of Saigon.

WHERE IS THE ENEMY

I didn't choose honey from your amphora as the first flavor
I've never known sleep free of cages
Night after night you rape the trembling animal
I spread zones of silence in your honor
Ready aim fire and false candor
You deflower my name in the name of your blood
I intone the last cry that terrifies the horses
The dust cures and comforts
I learned to shoot at an enemy   my motherland
I learned to shoot at an enemy   my body
I have been and will be an animal of obedience
I enter voluntarily into my cage and pose so as not to die
On my back another country flourishes
without owner or mandates
that country exists   purple sun that I long for
Broken knees   obedience from the budding girl
accusation written with blood
Who are we waiting for
Trained since infancy to find out
The red crosshair in the scope   the enemy advances
he disarms me and his strange likeness
to my father is surprising.

HAIKUBA

(SUMMER)

The last call sounds
I survive an eternal summer
we are preparing for something that is everything.

(WINTER)

The hibernating lotus awaits
the snow causes the tropics to fall ill
the girl's feet break the white bridges.

(CYCLONES)

Whom do we notify in case of an emergency?
I doodle on paper one hundred times a year
one day I'll draw your name in that empty space.

PLAYING HIDE AND SEEK

With my face buried in my arm   without cheating   with my back facing out
leaning against a tree   I counted to infinity while they hid
one one thousand   two one thousand   and when I opened my eyes   nighttime
Where is everyone?   So much time spent looking for them
One   two   three   four   five   six   seven   eight   nine   ten
How far away   how alone   how lost in the courtyard of my own game.

LOVERS IN A CRISIS

He's not the right man the one we choose in a crisis
a false stone   the bad copy
souls in diaspora
imitation of the treasure that is love
false body and false verb
A crisis is not the time for ever-after.

SNOW TOYS UNDER THE SUN

.

They won't knock on this door to play with me
neither king nor god nor magician who might surprise at dawn
Deserted toy stores
Pass through the dirty windowpanes   feel the smell of newness
gold   incense and myrrh   bait to my eyes
Toy tears twinkle on the sea
Where do my letters with drawings and pleas go?
I've already tasted the flavor of the water
No one will knock on this door to play with me.

BURDENS OF PINK SILK

Ballet toe shoe   pink shackle
Knife that bleeds my fears
Umbilical cord   outline of Cuba
Scribble and arrow   light when passed intoxicates
I twirl and I suffocate   I don't break the axis
Curled up in my suitcase
Anchored to the strings of my mother
Worn out naked feet
Ballet toe shoe that restricts my steps
Burden of volatile lead.

IN OTHER LANGUAGES

They've made her transparent
Vote of silence face-to-face with the painting
The ink is diluted in the sea of delusions
The women of the tropics don't cry
they smile   dance   enjoy themselves
A young girl swollen with pleasure carved her name
in the trunk of a tree
and the tree   moved deep in its bosom
let drop a flower for the young girl[1]
Sanity rubs against insanity
To forget the lyrics   the thread   the song
to leave one's mind
blank
to hold back one's breath
lethal exercise of apnea
To emerge in other languages
translated.

---

1 EUSEBIO DELFÍN

PENNILESS ORCHESTRA

Instruments that brush the past
caress and sing the loss
Guaguancó of linen and starch
pride of the arid province
Chords that jump flushed
The black man bundles up   he improvises a melody
the drums grieve   the pianos take pleasure
Bass in time   perfect   desperate trill
A drunk luthier cries on the bar
Guaguancó   red handkerchief   guayabera   languor and early morning
flavor of tamarind   dry wine   tobacco smoke
The rum maestro debuts his danzón
Far away village
with no way back
Penniless orchestra for hire on weekends
fleeting dance that the body performs by heart.

HOOK

We read to our parents in headlines of war
Sleeping guerrilleros   borrowed last names
We found our parents in fragile conditions
but we never discussed the rescue

Art schools were a mere refuge
that place where they let us be odd
We made communal love
jazzistas in a forced fusion

I don't fear suicide since strength has already abandoned me
breath that blows in favor of true freedom
Tattooed on my back is the name of lost poets
I am the bait on the hook that lured my mother away.

LE PUZZLE NOIR

In the house-home

Let someone watch over me as I sleep
rock me   calm me   guess my faith
Bull's eye   watches my terror
My demons fight they don't rest
The nightmare perfects itself and gains strength
The knife cuts the sea   it spreads it out unjustly
I was born black on a white tit
it feeds me and illustrates the innocence of the bird

Night   damp cloth that moistens and caresses
like a song in creole
doll pricked by pins
No one knows if I reveal water or poems
Being adopted is not strange
Being transplanted is dangerous
they change your name   your father   your life
I am going to recover in another being
rob spirits   last names   accents
The cages will not protect from the enlightened exterior
The cages NO
It smells like summer in Turkestan
white coffee   sedative and curative
The night keeps on scorching birds
false bonfires a place to die until morning.

STRETCHER MADE OF SALT

Asleep on the cement jacks   I cook my skin
I cure my head in the wave
It's not ephemeral art
these lives are not public interventions
strange world
nor tourists nor part of the west
The woman in the photo belongs to the official story
when I undress
I am reality
Read my scars exposed to the sun.

I'M SORRY FOR NOSOTROS

You don't use my perfume yet you carry my smell
You don't preserve my accent yet you bear my memories
I don't eat from your plate yet I miss the way you taste
I don't touch your body yet I bleed your wound
You don't speak from my mouth yet you say what I feel.

PLACEBOS

This rare inclination towards beauty
figurative
Dizzy spell between laughter and a smack
disguised
Feeling of oppression and pain
homicide
Fire-drill escape amongst islands and ruins
interiors
Confusion between motherland and government
sweet-and-sour
Intoxication and violence
endemic
Antidote and venom
diluted
Shipwreck in one's own land
a life preserver.

APPRENTICE TO HAIKU

Chiyo ni (千代尼)

paints what is happening

writes what no one can

lets herself get trapped by the kinetic state of tracing

She jumps with her small *jamo* net

she steadies herself before the indigo circle

she dies and is born

Without giving up the black chalk   she swims on the sand

Short stroke turned woman

she bows down to the nature of the occult

she intones a spiritual chant that eroticizes it

she offers herself up to the last reader   first lover

Her relationship takes place between desire and the word

She drinks slowly   she spills milk on the cloth

Verbal pause   the *kireji*   the island   the woman and the prey

knife   sun   girl   cradle   eternal summer that blesses us upon birth

Apprentice to Chiyo ni   my desire is to draw a brief winter

illustrating the body with questions

war that separates two contrasting images

poem that transpires on two shores divided by one soul.

Chiyo ni (千代尼)

The sun sleeps on top of the sun

I am not at peace.

ART OF THE REUNION

To make just in time the parts for a paper boat

The last call sounds at the wharf

I flee with the afternoon whistle

The wounds   before healing   should be named

What do we call that which hurts

Daño on paper

Everyone realizes when you are about to sail

I imagine leaving in a walnut shell

a net   a Chinese junk   a mad compass   the inventory of complaints

Newspapers with bad news make up the bow

Reinforced hypocrisy in red and black letters

water   oils   light food   medicine   mystic protection

There's a time in childhood when they teach you about that magic art

of paper a way out toward your hands

the making of a suicide toy

you sail in a circle   they break your boat   you don't return from your dream

Death awaits at the bottom of ink-stained paper

Life is the text

wet headline

news story written on paper for boats

The last call was made on ink.

HONEY

One never knows what flows under the river

I felt Oshún lay down at my side
fanning with her five skirts
she danced to the murmur of my luck
I sang my fears   fertility and abandonment
playing like little girls
we lost ourselves in feminine prayer
I confessed how much I have lied or they have lied to me
offerings and chants healed my dazed head
I prayed for health to delight in the treasures of the body
She clarified ideas   I guide my shadow without declaring the danger
I asked if my path was made of rocks or letters
obsidian   coal   white ashes   short-lived orchids   stale bread or will-o'-the-wisp
I lowered myself into the swirling spring
and I surrendered   guilty heart
my only crown I left in the river
Queen who placates the storm in lust
a barefoot plebian makes an offering.

Broken warriors rose up through her grace
she saved the world flying high   transformed into a vulture
She asked for the earth when Olokun sent the flood
Proprietress of the gold   the honeys and the faith   she dances dressed in yellow
recognizing valor as the only merit
She reigns here   the only orisha *who kills with her laugh*

She too wandered lost   hungry and alone like ribbon in the wind
Five skirts smeared
white and black women drink her honey
females and men sense the celebrations
Water on water   her tears cleansed the dress
She knew as well what it was to walk alone and barefoot
she found the path between the boulders
Oshún   illuminated by the gods
Oshún   wife of the warrior
Sunflower and miracle   birth and cinnamon

Oshún the poor one   the beautiful one   the smiling one
wise female   mother that lives in the river.

Barefoot   opening threshers   soul that guides desire
faithful to Eleggua   king crowned by Africa
wife of Shangó   saintly virile warrior
rattles magic and delirium
Sister and strand of water   the profound Yemayá.

Oshún travels far and lights up the paths
she sparks quarrels between orisha and men
she alleviates misunderstandings with her grace

Oshún's fan cures

Calms
intones
dispossesses
perfumes
invigorates

I opened my eyes the river coursed over my body
I saw the traps fall   forlorn   disintegrated
She too walked free and alone   like ribbon in the wind
My clothes were dirty   my soul was not.

LEGACY OF THE TEA

I've taken the place of my grandmother in this funeral
My sister will occupy the spot of my mother
feeble creature who drags her black kimono on her shoulders
she escapes history
she puts an end to the eternal nodding of "yes"
Over the tea sweet liquors are poured
sugars intoxications flattery and pleasure
rite that initiates and dismisses the veterans
I've taken the place of my grandmother
conqueror of black islands
even dead she continues to rule
I will trace my word   I will change the sound
I've taken with one gulp the place of my grandmother
I practice her calligraphy with raised hand
I caress the message that all want to receive
I read my palms I decipher desire I observe and wait
in my place there is no one
Heiress of the tea and its powers I remember and wait
My sister cries protected under the parasols
My mother apportions the guilt and the jewels
I've taken the place of my grandmother in this black fiesta
After centuries of listening to her version of the tea
my written word on paper is "no."

TWO GIRLS IN ONE BODY

Dark part of the night   when the lighthouse sleeps
The music makes you dizzy
The filigree lights at the port extinguished
The blackouts progress down the guarded coasts
My mother has stopped smoking in the armoire
Underneath the sheet my phosphorescence burns
The daughter switches on the flashlight and blinds me
Fear shakes the bed
I respond with terror
Games with lights   farewells   warnings from the body
final glimmers from my childhood
Girls who pass each other in the night.

THE DAUGHTER IN HER CAGE

I sold ice to the Eskimos and sand to the Arabs
but they never treated me like a real person
I don't ask for loans   I'm not guilty   I don't listen to insults
Offences sound like petals on snow
I use gloves so as not to touch the grand floating Steinway that is Cuba
They accept me without excusing my true spite
Even if I steal kill save or cure   I plot suicide with glass and thirst
in a misreading of the text
the letter that translates my body and other lances is mistaken
I am my character   to whom I commend myself   in whom   I take shelter
Trained to act   without snares or hiding places
Trained to pay last respects and bury in cold blood   I confess
The genius is my mother and her design promises more and more cages
Sequences of her reclaimed memory
Her daughter acts naked   in the cage   with a view of beyond

Wendy Guerra grew up in Cienfuegos, Cuba. Well known in Latin America and Europe, her previous books include the award winning *Platea A Oscoras, Cabeza Rapada, Ropa Interior,* and *Todos Se Van / Everyone Leaves.*

Elizabeth Polli's recent publications include translations of poetry, prose and essays by Sergio Chejfec, Felix de la Concha, Fritz Glockner, Ana Merino, José María Merio and Luis Muñoz. She is currently working on a novel by Wendy Guerra. Her translations of scholarly essays on comics have also appeared in the "International Journal of Comic Art". Currently Polli is the Spanish Language Program Director at Dartmouth College, where she has taught and directed the Spanish language program since 1998.